ANAHEIM DUCKS

BY DAVID J. CLARKE

Book design by Maggie Villaume
Cover design by Maggie Villaume

Photographs ©: John Minchillo/AP Images, cover; Alex Gallardo/AP Images, 4–5; Jeffrey T. Barnes/AP Images, 6; Jeff McIntosh/The Canadian Press/AP Images, 8; Elsa Hasch/Allsport/Getty Images Sport/Getty Images, 10–11; Bill Janscha/AP Images, 12; Paul Sakuma/AP Images, 14; Mark Avery/AP Images, 16–17, 20; Chris Carlson/AP Images, 19, 23; Carlos Osorio/AP Images, 24–25; Mark J. Terrill/AP Images, 27; Jae C. Hong/AP Images, 29

Press Box Books, an imprint of Press Room Editions.

ISBN
978-1-63494-671-1 (library bound)
978-1-63494-695-7 (paperback)
978-1-63494-741-1 (epub)
978-1-63494-719-0 (hosted ebook)

Library of Congress Control Number: 2022919608

Distributed by North Star Editions, Inc.
2297 Waters Drive
Mendota Heights, MN 55120
www.northstareditions.com

Printed in the United States of America
Mankato, MN
082023

ABOUT THE AUTHOR

David J. Clarke is a freelance sportswriter. Originally from Helena, Montana, he now lives in Savannah, Georgia, with his golden retriever, Gus.

TABLE OF
CONTENTS

1

Trevor Zegras was named to the All-Rookie Team for the 2021–22 season.

TREVOR
TERRIFIC

naheim Ducks winger Rickard Rakell dumped a backhand pass behind the opposing net. Teammate Trevor Zegras was waiting for it. And once Zegras had the puck, anything could happen.

Zegras paused for a moment. The center was all alone. Ducks teammate Sonny Milano was camped out in front of the net. But three Buffalo Sabres defenders surrounded him. Sliding a pass to

Trevor Zegras scoops the puck onto his stick blade against the Buffalo Sabres.

Milano was too risky. Zegras had another idea. The former first-round draft pick was known for his creativity. And he was about to show just how much of it he had.

Zegras curled the blade of his stick around the puck to scoop it up. The puck seemed stuck to his stick. Then he gently tossed the puck to Milano beside the net. Milano was ready for it. He swung his stick at the puck and smacked it out of midair. The puck sailed past the Buffalo goaltender for an incredible goal.

Milano charged around the net to celebrate. Zegras waited for him with his hands on his head. His stunned look told the story. Even he couldn't believe what the two players had just done.

The goal was reviewed. The officials wanted to make sure Milano's stick was not above the crossbar. That would have made the play illegal. While the officials

Sonny Milano tallied 34 points during the 2021–22 season.

checked the video, the TV announcer begged for the goal to count, just because the play was "so cool." Fortunately for Ducks fans, the goal stood.

The Ducks fell short of the playoffs in 2021–22. It was their fourth straight year out of the postseason. But Ducks fans knew their team had great young talent. And they knew their newest star was capable of magic.

•DO THE MICHIGAN

Two months after Trevor Zegras's "lacrosse pass" to Sonny Milano, he used the same move to score. The goal came against the Montreal Canadiens on January 27, 2022. Goals like that are known as "Michigan" goals in hockey. That is because of Mike Legg. In 1996, the University of Michigan forward became the first player to pull the move off in a game.

2

Steve Rucchin
played for the
Mighty Ducks
for ten seasons
from 1994–95 to
2003–04.

HOLLYWOOD ORIGIN

Southern California has always been known for movies. Many of its most famous films have been created by the Walt Disney Company. In 1992, Disney put out a film called *The Mighty Ducks*. The story followed a youth hockey team in Minnesota.

At the same time, the company was buying a new National Hockey League (NHL) franchise. The new team would play in Anaheim.

Paul Kariya scored 300 goals in his nine seasons with Anaheim.

Its rink would be just down the road from Disneyland. And Disney decided to name the team after the movie. That is how the Mighty Ducks of Anaheim were born in 1993.

Like the team in the film, the Mighty Ducks struggled at first. It took Anaheim four years to make the playoffs. Star forwards Paul Kariya and Teemu Selänne led the turnaround. Both were among the league's best scorers in 1996–97. Anaheim won its first playoff series that spring. In the first round, the Mighty Ducks defeated the Phoenix Coyotes in seven games. Goaltender Guy Hebert recorded Anaheim's first playoff shutout in Game 7.

Anaheim did not win another playoff series for six years. But in 2003, the Mighty Ducks went on a run to the Stanley Cup Final. Anaheim's run started with upsets of the Detroit Red Wings and the Dallas Stars. Both teams were huge

Jean-Sébastien Giguère had a save percentage of .945 in the 2003 playoffs.

favorites. Goalie Jean Sébastien Giguère was outstanding in the playoffs. In the conference final, he allowed just one goal as Anaheim swept Minnesota. He posted five shutouts during the playoffs.

The Ducks' run finally ended in the Stanley Cup Final. The New Jersey Devils won the series in seven games.

A RARE HONOR

The Conn Smythe Trophy is given every year to the Most Valuable Player (MVP) in the Stanley Cup playoffs. It almost always goes to a player on the winning team. Jean-Sébastien Giguère took home the award in 2003. He was the fifth player to win it on a team that did not win the Cup.

3

Teemu Selänne spent 15 seasons of his Hall of Fame career in Anaheim.

FLYING HIGH

In 2005, Disney decided to sell the Mighty Ducks. The new owners made some changes. In 2006, they changed the team's uniform colors. Teal and purple were out. The new look was orange and black. The owners also shortened the name. Now the team would be known simply as the Anaheim Ducks.

Whatever they were called, they were good. The Ducks went

12–0–4 to start the 2006–07 season. Anaheim set team records with 48 wins and 110 points. Teemu Selänne led the offense with 48 goals. Jean-Sébastien Giguère was solid in goal. And the Ducks had two of the league's best defensemen. Scott Niedermayer was the team captain. Chris Pronger was an offensive threat and physical on defense.

The Ducks were unstoppable in the playoffs. They lost only four games in the first three rounds. Two 22-year-olds led the way. Center Ryan Getzlaf had a team-high 17 playoff points. Winger Corey Perry added 15.

Anaheim met the Ottawa Senators in the Stanley Cup Final. The Ducks won

Chris Pronger celebrates scoring a goal in a 2006 game against the New York Islanders.

three of the first four games, each by one goal. In Game 5, Andy McDonald scored less than four minutes in for the Ducks. It was the start of a great team performance.

Scott Niedermayer lifts the Stanley Cup in 2007.

In the second period, a strange play helped Anaheim. Ottawa defenseman Chris Phillips picked up the puck behind his net. As he moved forward, he got tangled up with Ottawa goalie Ray Emery. The puck bounced off Emery's skate and into the net. Travis Moen was the last Anaheim player to touch the puck. That meant he got credit for the goal. It ended up being the score that clinched the Stanley Cup.

The Ducks skated away with a 6–2 victory. Niedermayer won the Conn Smythe Trophy. Just minutes after hoisting that trophy, the captain got to lift the Cup.

•WEST COAST TITLE

The 2006–07 Ducks were the first team from California to win the Stanley Cup. In fact, until 2007, only three other West Coast teams had ever done it. The Vancouver Millionaires did it first in 1915. The Seattle Metropolitans in 1917 and the Victoria Cougars in 1925 were the others.

RYAN GETZLAF

Ducks coach Randy Carlyle decided to team up three of his youngest players in the 2007 playoffs. He put together a line with Dustin Penner and Corey Perry on the wings. In the center was Ryan Getzlaf. All three forwards were under 25. The "Kid Line" dominated as the Ducks claimed the Stanley Cup.

Getzlaf was the line's biggest star. He led the Ducks in scoring in those playoffs. Getzlaf was a physical force. But he was also one of the game's best passers. He led the Ducks in assists for 13 straight seasons at one point.

In 2010, Getzlaf also took over leadership of the Ducks. He became the team captain when Scott Niedermayer retired. The center hung up his skates in 2022. Getzlaf ended his career as the team's all-time leader in games played, assists, and points.

Ryan Getzlaf registered more
than 1,000 points in his career.

4

Corey Perry scored more than 30 goals in six different seasons with the Ducks.

DUCK CALLS

As players like Scott Niedermayer and Teemu Selänne got older, the Ducks began to struggle. It was time for new leaders to step up. In 2010, Ryan Getzlaf took over as the team captain. He and Corey Perry became an elite forward pair. They eventually became known as the "Twins" because they played together for so long.

The Twins had a new head coach in 2011. Bruce Boudreau took over for Randy Carlyle. In 2013–14, his second full season, the Ducks won a team-record 54 games. But the playoffs were a letdown. Anaheim lost in the second round.

A year later, the Ducks rolled through the first two rounds. Then they faced the Chicago Blackhawks in the conference finals. The series was filled with tight games. In Game 5, Anaheim forward Matt Beleskey scored an overtime winner.

A HART FOR PERRY

Corey Perry had a career year in 2010–11. He led the league with 50 goals. That included 11 game winners. After scoring 98 points, Perry won the Hart Memorial Trophy. The award is given to the NHL's MVP. Perry became the first Ducks player to win it.

Matt Beleskey celebrates his overtime winner against Chicago in the 2015 conference finals.

That put Anaheim up 3–2 in the series. But the Ducks couldn't close it out. Chicago won the next two games on its way to a Stanley Cup title.

Two years later, Carlyle came back to coach Anaheim. He immediately led the Ducks back to the conference finals. This time, Anaheim was defeated by the Nashville Predators in six games.

After that, the Ducks began to struggle. Perry left after the 2018–19 season. Getzlaf retired three years later. He had played all 17 years of his career in Anaheim. The Ducks fell short of the 2019 playoffs. That began a new streak of missing the postseason. The team still had star goalie John Gibson, but he needed help. When young players like Trevor Zegras showed up in 2021, Ducks fans hoped more success was on the way.

John Gibson's 2.07 goals-against average in 2015–16 was the best single-season mark in team history.

• ANAHEIM DUCKS
QUICK STATS

TEAM HISTORY: Mighty Ducks of Anaheim (1993–2006), Anaheim Ducks (2007–)

STANLEY CUP CHAMPIONSHIPS: 1 (2007)

KEY COACHES:

- Mike Babcock (2002–04): 69 wins, 62 losses, 19 ties, 14 overtime losses
- Randy Carlyle (2005–11, 2016–19): 384 wins, 256 losses, 96 overtime losses
- Bruce Boudreau (2011–16): 208 wins, 104 losses, 40 overtime losses

HOME ARENA: Honda Center (Anaheim, CA)

MOST CAREER POINTS: Ryan Getzlaf (1,019)

MOST CAREER GOALS: Teemu Selänne (457)

MOST CAREER ASSISTS: Ryan Getzlaf (737)

MOST CAREER SHUTOUTS: Jean-Sébastien Giguère (32)

Stats are accurate through the 2021–22 season.

GLOSSARY

ASSISTS
Passes, rebounds, or deflections that result in goals.

BLADE
The part of the stick that handles the puck.

CAPTAIN
A team's leader.

CONFERENCE
A smaller group of teams that make up part of a sports league.

DRAFT
An event that allows teams to choose new players coming into the league.

ELITE
One of the best.

OVERTIME
One or more extra periods played after regulation if a game is still tied.

SWEEP
When a team wins all the games in a series.

TO LEARN MORE

BOOKS

Berglund, Bruce. *Big-Time Hockey Records*. North Mankato, MN: Capstone Press, 2022.

Doeden, Matt. *G.O.A.T. Hockey Teams*. Minneapolis: Lerner Publications, 2021.

Nicks, Erin. *NHL*. Minneapolis: Abdo Publishing, 2021.

MORE INFORMATION

To learn more about the Anaheim Ducks, go to **pressboxbooks.com/AllAccess**.

These links are routinely monitored and updated to provide the most current information available.

INDEX